Menstruation:
Just Plain Talk

Menstruation: Just Plain Talk

by Alan E. Nourse, M.D.

Franklin Watts
New York/London/Toronto/Sydney/1980
A First Book

The author's thanks go to
Bev, Liu Tang, Marge,
Mary, Sara, and Sharon
for sharing their experiences.

Diagrams by Vantage Art, Inc.

Library of Congress Cataloging in Publication Data

Nourse, Alan Edward.
Menstruation, just plain talk.

(A First book)
Includes index.
SUMMARY: Discusses the menstrual cycle,
abnormalities and their treatment, and the
significance of menstruation in one's life.
1. Menstruation—Juvenile literature.
2. Menstruation disorders—Juvenile literature.
[1. Menstruation] I. Title.
RG161.N59   612'.662   80–14868
ISBN 0–531–04164–6

10

Contents

Menstruation: Just Plain Talk

Foreword

The first menstrual period has always been a very important event in the life of the adolescent girl. In the days of our grandmothers and great-grandmothers, little was known about how a woman's body functioned; consequently, there were many myths and misconceptions surrounding this event. Very often the happiness and pride which should be evident upon reaching this milestone on the path toward becoming an adult were distorted by the secrecy surrounding menstruation and the fear caused by insufficient knowledge of normal bodily processes. Many girls quickly learned that most adults, including mothers and doctors, felt very uncomfortable discussing menstruation. Their questions went unasked and unanswered. Often this secrecy was perpetuated because of the unproven belief that by informing teenagers about their developing bodies, one might somehow encourage sexual experimentation.

We now know that information is not as dangerous as ignorance. The more we know and understand about how our bodies work, the easier it is to care for them wisely and well. Today, people of all ages are much healthier and live longer than in grandmother's day. This fortunate state of affairs is partially due to the vast increase in medical knowledge that has occurred during this century. We have every reason to believe that as women become more informed and less ashamed of the complex and wonderful workings of their bodies, they will become healthier in all aspects of their lives, both physically and emotionally.

However, gaining information about her body and her feelings is not an easy task for the young adolescent. She must gain this information at a time when she is trying to achieve some independence from her parents as well as from other adults. This normal and very necessary process of separation from family, which begins in early adolescence, places a strain upon the usual lines of communication between parent and child. Parents must learn to convey information in a manner which allows these emerging adults to make some of their own decisions. Similarly, teenagers must somehow learn just when they are truly capable of making intelligent judgments and when they are still in need of informed adult advice. This delicate balance is even more precarious when the issues to be learned and discussed deal with developing sexuality. Often their own fears and lack of information lead parents to avoid discussion of this sensitive area. Further, a developing sense of privacy and embarrassment regarding sexual issues may steer the teenager away from the support of even the most understanding parents.

Menstruation: Just Plain Talk has a significant role to play in this common family situation. It allows the teenage girl to inform herself and find answers to her questions about her body and menstruation in a private and independent way. It encourages her to accept responsibility for understanding how her body functions and how to care for it. The book provides an excellent introduction to the fascinating workings of the female body. There is a clear, accurate description of the normal processes of adolescence including an explanation of the events occurring during a menstrual cycle. Both common normal variations and abnormal situations are discussed in a way that will help the teenager decide which occurrences might require medical attention. Current approaches to treatment of abnormal situations are outlined in a manner which allows for easy understanding by the young reader.

One of the most helpful aspects of this book is that it emphasizes the proper vocabulary for describing puberty and menstruation. We are told the names of the important glands, organs, and hormones and are even given the historical derivation of some of these words. As a first step toward understanding any new subject, the vocabulary is essential. After reading this book, teenagers will be able to ask their questions and discuss their concerns with more confidence and accuracy.

I would highly recommend this book to all young teenagers and their parents. The information presented is simple, clear and up-to-date. When read by parent and child this book will serve not as a substitute for discussion but rather as a stimulus to the exchange of information and feelings between parent and adolescent.

Susan Coupey, M.D.
Division of Adolescent Medicine
Montefiore Hospital and Medical Center
Bronx, New York

Chapter One:
What's Going On?

For virtually every girl reading this book, there will come a day in her early teenage years when she reaches a major turning point in her physical life, the day she first begins menstruating.

What exactly is **menstruation?** In plainest possible terms, it is a flow of blood and cell fragments that passes from the interior of the **uterus,** or womb, down the **vagina** to the outside of the body at more or less regular intervals. Menstrual periods, or just plain **periods,** usually begin in the early teenage years and continue until a woman is about forty or fifty years old. The word *menstruation* actually comes from the Latin word *mensa,* meaning "month," since the average interval from the start of one menstrual period to the start of the next is about twenty-eight days, roughly a month according to the ancient Roman calendar.

Doctors call the flow itself **menses.** It usually lasts from four to six days, a little less for some, a little more for others. A girl's very first menstrual period is called her **menarche** (pronounced men AR key). The girl's periods will not normally be suspended, then, except during pregnancies, until she reaches **menopause,** or "end of menstruation," many years later.

No one can say exactly when your menstrual periods will begin. For some of you, they will already have started; for others not yet. Menarche is determined to some extent by heredity. In addition, certain physical signs, such as breast enlargement and the appearance of body hair in places where it wasn't previously, usually precede the onset of menstruation by about one and a half to two and a half years. But no matter when your menstruation does begin, it is an outward and obvious sign that some very striking changes are going on inside your physically maturing body.

Menstruation may appear suddenly, but it is not something that just suddenly happens, like the snapping of the fingers or the blinking of an eye. Rather, it is the last in a long series of chemical and biological events, events that begin months or even years before the first menstruation occurs. Starting to menstruate is an important sign of **puberty,** that time of life during which a person's mature sexual self emerges. But it is only one such sign.

Perhaps you have already read some things about menstruation. Perhaps you have attended a health or hygiene course or seen a movie at school. Certainly, many of you will have talked to your mothers, older sisters, or friends about the subject. But chances are that the whole business of menstruation is still somewhat unclear, puzzling, maybe even frightening to many of you. What's going on? Why menstruation, of all things?

There is usually no need for apprehension about menstruation. Yet sometimes seemingly odd and different things do happen, and when they do, questions arise.

THREE GIRLS
Let's consider the very different things that happened to three girls, whose names have been changed but whose stories are based on actual experiences.

• To her mother's considerable distress, Janie McC. began her first menstrual period just three weeks after her ninth birthday. Both she and her mother had noticed a considerable amount of breast enlargement for some months before the menstrual period occurred. This sign of sexual maturity had already upset Janie's mother, who felt that it was beginning unusually early. But when Janie's menstruation began before she was even ten years old, her mother promptly took her to the doctor. What was going on here?

• Karen K.'s story was quite different. Karen began her first menstrual period just before her thirteenth birthday—exactly when you might expect it to occur—but then she didn't have another period for eight solid months. When it finally did come, her second period was so very scant that it hardly seemed like a period at all. Then again, months passed without any further menstruation. Finally, convinced that something was terribly wrong, Karen's mother took her to see the doctor. What was going on?

• At least Karen K. did have a menstrual period at about the time in her life when it was expected. Pamela C. did not. Although other signs of sexual maturity began appearing when she was thirteen or fourteen years old, Pamela still had not had a menstrual period of any sort by the time she was sixteen. She seemed perfectly well and happy, and she objected to being bothered with a visit to the doctor, but her mother insisted. What was going on?

In fact, nothing terribly unusual was going on with any one of these three girls. True enough, Janie's sexual maturity and the beginning of her menstrual period came surprisingly early. But, as her doctor explained, it was still at the early edge of the normal age range when these events can occur. While *most* girls begin their periods sometime between age eleven and age fourteen, there are a few who start earlier and a few who start later. Of course Janie's doctor took a careful medical history, looking for any sign of possible trouble, and performed a thorough physical examination. In addition, he collected a blood sample, to be tested for certain chemical imbalances and to be as certain as he could that Janie was not suffering from some rare condition. But, as he had expected, nothing abnormal was found. Janie McC. was in the peak of good health, had nothing wrong with her, and was simply one of three or four percent of all girls who begin menstruating very early.

Normal good health was the doctor's verdict for Karen K. as well. After performing a simple physical exam to assure himself of this fact, he explained to Karen and her mother that while many girls who begin menstruating at the age of thirteen or so proceed to have an orderly and regular schedule of menstrual periods right from the start, many others do not. Indeed, the doctor said, it was perfectly normal for a girl to have as much as a year or two of irregular periods before a regular pattern became established. The doctor said he would not advise any treatment at this time. He added that if Karen's irregular periods continued beyond what he deemed normal, treatment was available and might at that time be advisable. In this case, however, treatment did not prove necessary. Karen had a third and normal menstrual period soon after her visit to the doctor and had a fourth a month later. Her periods remained somewhat unpredictable and irregular for another year, but they gradually settled down to a reliable twenty-six-day interval and remained that way from then on.

Pamela C.'s situation seemed a bit more mysterious to her doctor until he learned one vital fact about her life: Pamela, it turned out, was an extraordinarily active young woman. She was, in fact, deeply involved in gymnastics, one of the most brutally demanding and strenuous of all athletic activities. Pamela had been attending a special gymnastics school and was being privately coached as well. She was spending as much as six to eight hours a day in the gymnasium, day after day, developing her strength, timing, precision, and physical control.

The doctor pointed out that this excessive activity might well be delaying Pamela's menstruation. Recent scientific studies, he said, had shown that girls who are engaged in extreme physical activity over prolonged periods quite often begin menstruating later than other girls. There were other differences, too. Such girls often do not gain the height or weight that most teenage girls do in the months before menstruation. Of course, the doctor said, these girls do catch up sooner or later. Very often when they take a lengthy vacation from their physical activity or catch a bad case of flu and have to rest for a while, they suddenly begin menstruating.

FANTASIES
AND FAIRYTALES

Clearly menstruation can vary a great deal from one person to another and still fall within the normal range. Equally clearly, menstruation is a normal bodily function of girls who are maturing sexually. You might think that anything so normal and so commonplace—after all, half the people in the world have periodic menstruation throughout a large part of their lives—would simply be accepted by everyone as okay, natural, even rather nice, a sign that things are going the way they are supposed to.

Actually, attitudes toward menstruation could not be more opposite. Until very recently, any mention of menstruation was considered thoroughly taboo—forbidden—except in very private and embarrassed circumstances. In fact, throughout most of history, menstruation has been regarded with apprehension, shame, embarrassment, and distress. It has been the cause of innumerable social rules that have restricted the lives and activities of young women everywhere and the subject of all sorts of ridiculous folk tales, beliefs, and scare stories, virtually all of them untrue. What is more, many of these restrictive rules, practices, and foolish stories remain active even today.

You may have already noticed, for example, that almost nobody refers to menstruation by its actual name. Any number of other words are used instead. Often you will hear it called "the curse," based upon the idea that it is a sort of woman's burden. Other times you may hear it called "the friend," perhaps referring to the fact that the beginning of a menstrual flow is a sign that a woman is not pregnant, and thus the period's appearance is greeted with relief by a woman who has been worried about this. Some girls have their own private names that they use based on purely personal experience. Other terms, such as "falling off the roof" or "falling out of bed" defy explanation.

Just as there are many names for menstruation that suggest it is something shameful or disgusting, there are any number of strange and curious beliefs about this natural bodily function that suggest there is something wrong with a woman who is menstruating. Even today there are people who believe that a menstruating woman will cause milk to sour, wine to turn to vinegar, the leaves of houseplants to droop, or cut flowers to wilt. Innumerable girls believe that they smell bad during menstruation, which is totally untrue as long as they pay normal attention to their physical cleanliness. Others mistakenly believe that to skip a period means serious physical harm because it keeps in bad blood that needs to come out. Girls beyond number have been carefully taught that to go swimming during a menstrual period is practically sudden death and that physical activity during a period should be severely restricted. Some girls really believe that the only thing to do during their period is to go to bed with a cold towel on their foreheads.

Even worse, a number of girls approaching their first period are secretly terrified by stories they have heard about extreme blood loss, agonizing pain, or terrible physical impairment of some sort. Far more come to think of menstruation as a *mal*function of their bodies, something that is somehow shameful and too awful to think about. Still other girls have been told that to menstruate means you are a woman, and they are frightened because they don't understand what this involves.

Many of these negative attitudes and feelings that put down or degrade menstruation have their roots in cultures or religions thousands of years old. Two hundred years ago, long before disposable pads were even thought of to control menses in a convenient and sanitary manner, women in parts of Italy were being taught that to even mention they were menstruating was wrong. These women used cloths to absorb their flow, and they had to hide the cloths in cracks in the wall until they could later secretly wash them for reuse. Many societies associated pain, distress, and disgust with menstruation. Some primitive tribes forced women to remain alone in their huts during the menstrual periods. Natives of the Aleutian Islands would not allow a menstruating female near the water, for fear that she would spoil the fishing.

In ancient Hebrew societies, a woman was regarded as sexually "unclean" during her period plus an interval of seven days after her flow had stopped. During that time she and her husband were not permitted to have sexual relations nor to sleep in the same bed. They were not even supposed to touch each other. At the end of the seven days, the woman would immerse herself in a river or lake or special indoor pool as a purification ritual. Similar practices persist even to this day in many Jewish communities around the world.

Society's restrictive rules disappear very slowly. And with so many strange beliefs, stories, and myths having grown up around menstruation, it is hardly any wonder that so many girls are still in the dark as to what is *really* going on. Why does menstruation occur in the first place? What is true about it and what is not? To find clear, understandable answers we first need some basic facts about the events that occur in a girl's body as she approaches sexual maturity—events that ultimately lead to menstruation.

Chapter Two:
Just the Facts, Ma'am

As we said earlier, menstruation is not something that just suddenly happens. It is the last in a long series of chemical and biological events, and every one of those events depends upon the action of chemical substances in the body called **hormones.** Thus, before we can understand what menstruation is all about, we must first know something about what these hormones do.

PREPARING FOR REPRODUCTION
Actually, menstruation is just one rather minor part of a much larger bodily function known as the **female reproductive cycle,** every part of which is controlled from the start by the action of certain hormones.

Hormones are powerful chemical substances produced in the body in special organs called **glands.** Sometimes we speak of hormones as chemical messengers, or chemicals that act at a distance. This is because most hormones (including many that are concerned with reproduction) are produced in glands in one part of the body and then travel by way of the bloodstream to other, distant organs to bring about their effect. However, some of the most important hormones involved in human reproduction are produced in the so-called **sex glands,** which in the female are the **ovaries** and in the male are the **testicles.** Still other reproductive hormones are produced in the outer shell, or cortex, of the **adrenal glands,** which sit perched like little caps on top of the kidneys. Finally, many important reproductive hormones are formed in the **pituitary gland,** a tiny gland that lies deep inside the skull at the base of the brain.

Oddly enough, the first effects these reproductive hormones have don't really have very much to do with reproduction at all —at least not directly. Just as the soil in a field must be prepared before wheat can grow in it, the body must be prepared before it can ultimately become capable of reproduction. The first reproductive hormone activities are, in a sense, preparing the ground for things that will happen later.

Consider first what happens to a girl as she approaches her twelfth birthday. Most girls at the age of nine or ten closely resemble boys of the same age in physical size and shape. They tend to be thin, flat-chested, and gangly. They are all bones and angles. Their bodies are largely hairless except for the hair on their heads, and their voices have just about the same pitch. Many girls in this age group engage and compete in the same sports and physical activities as boys, enjoy the same games, and play—or fight—with boys on pretty even ground.

Sooner or later, however, certain differences begin to appear.

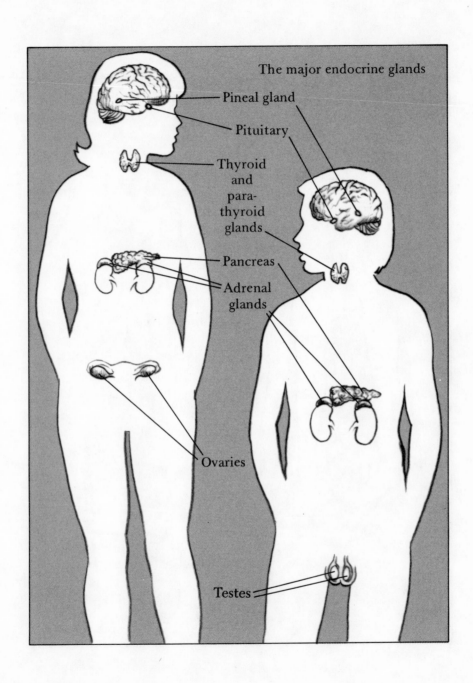

The major endocrine glands

Pineal gland

Pituitary

Thyroid
and
para-
thyroid
glands

Pancreas

Adrenal
glands

Ovaries

Testes

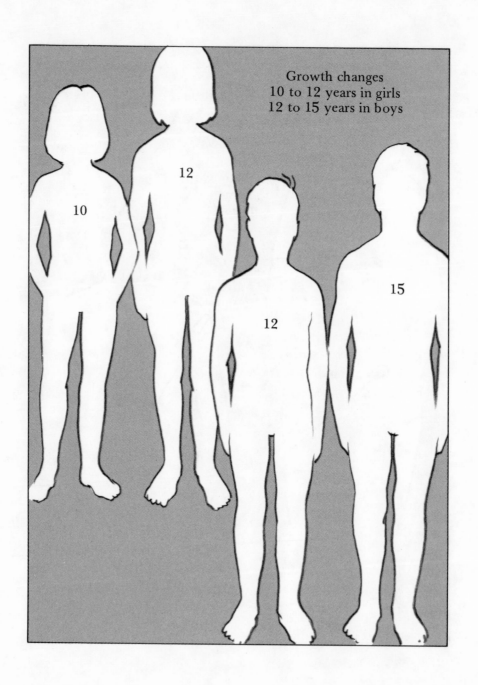

Growth changes
10 to 12 years in girls
12 to 15 years in boys

10

12

12

15

At about age eleven or twelve, sometimes a little earlier, sometimes a little later, a girl undergoes a sudden surge of physical growth. She becomes taller. Her bones become longer and heavier, and she develops larger and stronger muscles than before. In some girls this so-called **growth spurt** is so quiet and subtle that it is hardly even noticed; in others it may be quite marked. In either case, the end of this period of growth will determine how tall and heavy-boned the girl will be throughout the rest of her life.

During the growth spurt, signs of sexual maturity are also beginning to appear. The girl's breasts begin to enlarge and will continue to develop for a period of two to three years. Pubic hair begins to appear between the legs. Hair also starts to grow under the arms. The girl will develop a layer of fat on the shoulders and hips that will change her "string bean" appearance to a more rounded or curvy shape. Although her voice will not change sharply, it will usually become more mature and less babyish than it was before. Finally, the girl may find herself becoming more interested in boys as *boys* rather than just as competitors on the baseball field.

THE SECONDARY
SEX CHARACTERISTICS

All these changes are primarily the work of certain female sex hormones that have begun to be produced in the girl's ovaries. The most important of these hormones are called **estrogens,** meaning, literally, "estrus-makers," a term that applies to periods of special sexual readiness or "heat" common to female dogs, cats, and other lower animals. Human females have no such special intervals reserved for sexual activity, but the term seems to have stuck.

Doctors speak of these physical changes as **secondary sex characteristics** because none of them is directly involved with

[17]

reproduction at all—at first. Yet they do prepare the girl's body in some important ways for a pregnancy.

Of course boys, too, develop secondary sex characteristics. The growth spurt in boys, usually occurring between ages twelve and fifteen, may be very striking, with as much as a foot (30 cm) or more in height gained in a matter of a year or two. The boy's bones become longer and heavier than the girl's, his muscles become more massive. He, too, develops underarm and pubic hair and his sexual organs become larger and more mature. (He will also start to grow a rudimentary beard and moustache, although this may be delayed for several years.) Because of a sudden enlargement in his larynx, or voice box, a boy's voice will drop to a lower register after an awkward period of adjustment. At this point, he, too, will be physically prepared for his mature reproductive function as a male.

The hormones that produce these male secondary sex characteristics are the so-called male sex hormones, or **androgens,** from Greek words meaning "man-maker." They are primarily produced in the testicles, although some are also produced in the adrenal glands. Actually, these so-called male and female sex hormones are by no means restricted to males or females respectively, as one might think. Although boys have a preponderance of androgens, their bodies also produce some estrogens. And while girls have predominantly estrogens, their bodies also produce small amounts of androgens. One proof of this fact is that most teenage girls suffer from that hated adolescent plague known as **acne,** or pimples, just as severely as boys do. But we know that the skin changes of acne are mainly a result of increased *androgen* activity in the body. A girl doesn't have to have very much androgen to stimulate acne; a little bit is all it takes. But if she had no androgens at all in her body, she would not develop acne.

[18]

THE OVULATION CYCLE

The secondary sex characteristics, in themselves, may not seem very important. They do result in girls beginning to look more like young women and boys beginning to look more like young men. And they do indicate that certain glands in the body are beginning to mature and produce male or female sex hormones in considerable quantity. They are a sign of approaching sexual maturity. But from nature's point of view, the whole idea of a girl or a boy becoming sexually mature is to make it possible for reproduction to take place—for a new human being to be formed. This requires a special cell—an egg cell, or **ovum** (pl. **ova**)—to be ripened and released in one of the girl's ovaries. The ovum carries half the hereditary information needed to create a new baby. Reproduction also requires the production of a special **sperm** cell in the young man's testicles—again a cell carrying half the hereditary information necessary to generate a new human baby. Boys begin to manufacture sperm during puberty and continue to do so for most of their lives. The special male and female reproductive cells normally meet as a result of sexual relations; in order for a pregnancy to occur, they must fuse together, or unite, in a process known as **fertilization.**

Sperm can be produced by the millions at almost any time, but nature is far more sparing in the production of ova. Ordinarily, ova are produced just one at a time, each one carefully prepared and released in the girl's body under the direction of special hormones. You might think of the production of each individual ovum as a major attempt on nature's part to make reproduction possible. If one attempt fails, nature makes another attempt, and then another and another in a recurring, repeated cycle that, once started, continues for some forty years.

From the time of birth on, a girl's ovaries contain many tiny, immature ova, just lying at rest. Each one of these immature ova

[19]

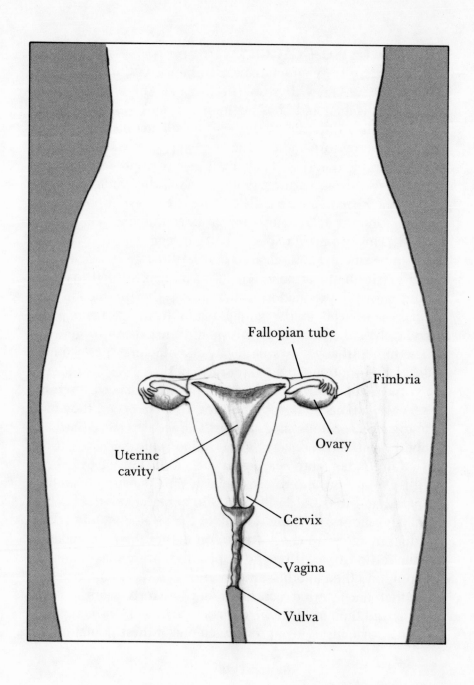

Fallopian tube

Fimbria

Ovary

Uterine
cavity

Cervix

Vagina

Vulva

is surrounded by a cluster or nest of protective cells. These microscopic nests are known as **follicles,** from the Latin word meaning "pod" or "shell." For the first ten years or so of a girl's life, none of these follicles changes much. Then at puberty, ranging from around age eleven to age twelve or thirteen, a special hormone is produced in larger amounts in the girl's pituitary gland and is released in tiny quantities into her bloodstream, where it travels to her ovaries. This hormone is the **follicle-stimulating hormone,** or **FSH.**

As you might guess from the name, the job of FSH is to stimulate the growth of cells in one single follicle, so that the ovum at that follicle's center will begin to enlarge and mature. But one hormone is not enough. After seven or eight days a second hormone from the pituitary gland appears and triggers the final enlargement and ripening of the ovum. Eventually the mature ovum breaks free from the follicle and is caught in the upper end of the **Fallopian tube** that is wrapped around the ovary. From there it is conducted slowly down into the upper end of the tube, where it can come in contact with a sperm cell and become fertilized. This process, the enlargement and release of an ovum into the Fallopian tube, is known as **ovulation,** and it is nature's grand attempt to make reproduction possible. As soon as the ovum is free from the follicle, that same second hormone that helped the process earlier immediately begins acting on the follicle cells left behind to form a small lump of pinkish-yellow tissue called the **corpus luteum** (from Latin words meaning "yellow body"). For that reason this second hormone is called **luteinizing hormone,** or **LH.**

Of course this new mature ovum will need a safe place to grow and develop if it becomes fertilized by the sperm. Again, it is hormones that set the stage. It takes about eight to ten days from the earliest ripening of an immature ovum to the time it is

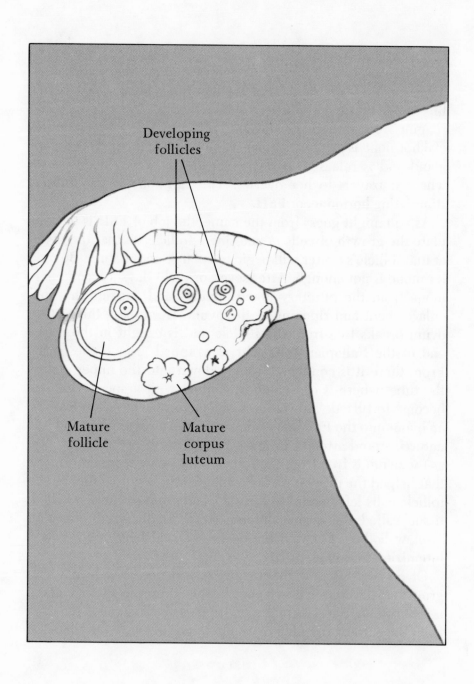

Developing
follicles

Mature
follicle

Mature
corpus
luteum

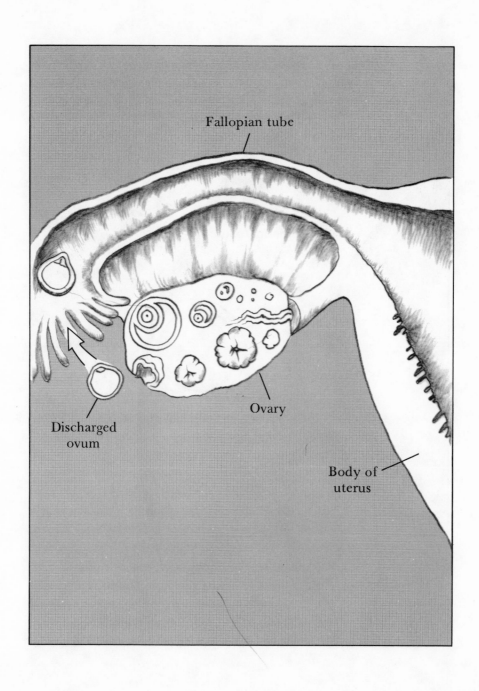

Fallopian tube

Ovary

Discharged
ovum

Body of
uterus

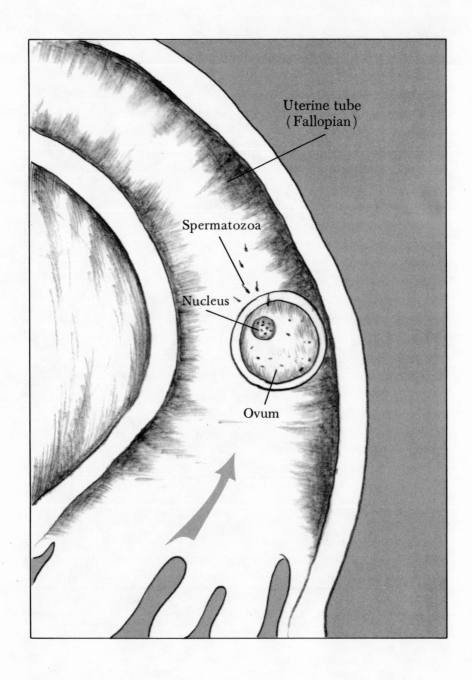

Uterine tube
(Fallopian)

Spermatozoa

Nucleus

Ovum

released. During that time, estrogens from the ovaries are very busy acting on cells lining the inside of the woman's uterus. The estrogens cause those cells to multiply very fast and to form special tiny blood vessels and tiny nurturing glands as they grow. By the time ovulation occurs, the uterine lining has become quite thick, with a rich blood supply. What is more, just after the ovum is released, that pinkish-yellow lump of tissue left behind in the ovary begins to produce a completely different hormone. Its job is to act on that enlarged lining of the uterus to make it soft and spongy and to make the glands begin to secrete sugars and other nutrients. This hormone is called **progesterone**, from Latin words meaning "ahead of pregnancy."

Last of all, yet another hormone, this one also from the pituitary gland, keeps prodding the corpus luteum to produce more and more progesterone, thus making sure that there is plenty of this "pregnancy-protecting" hormone around at the right time. Because this new hormone at a later stage works in partnership with estrogens to enlarge the woman's breasts and prepare them for milk production if she becomes pregnant, it is often called **lactogenic,** or "milk-producing," **hormone,** or simply **prolactin,** which means "before the milk."

All this may seem terribly complicated at first glance, but actually it makes perfect sense once you understand the point of it. The woman's body is making a grand attempt at reproduction, producing a mature ovum ready to be fertilized and, at the same time, preparing a safe place for it to lodge and grow into a baby should it become fertilized. In order to accomplish these things a whole series of events has taken place, each event directed by a special hormone. And with one possible exception, there is no clue or signal to tell the woman that any of these hormone-directed activities is taking place. Once in a while, in some women, a bit of fluid may escape into the abdomen just

[25]

when the ripened ovum breaks free from its follicle, and this fluid may cause some twinges of discomfort in the lower abdomen right at ovulation time. This discomfort, called **mittelschmerz,** a German word meaning "pain in the middle," can give the woman a clue that ovulation has taken place. But since it only happens to some women, and then only sometimes, it cannot be taken as a reliable signal of ovulation. In addition, very careful measurement of the body's temperature may reveal a slight temperature increase when ovulation takes place. But the average person would find measuring this difference very difficult. In general, then, this sequence of events simply provides no reliable clues.

ENTER MENSTRUATION

Obviously, up until ovulation, nothing is decided as far as nature's attempt at reproduction is concerned. It is during ovulation that the all-important step takes place. At that time a particular ovum can meet up with a sperm cell and become fertilized. But if it does not, within a matter of just forty-eight hours or so the ovum will simply disintegrate. The corpus luteum will begin to shrink and stop producing progesterone. Several days later the specially prepared lining of the uterus, with its glands and many small blood vessels, will begin to break down. A quantity of cellular material and a certain amount of blood will then pass down through the lower end of the uterus, known as the **cervix,** and be carried out of the body by way of the vagina in a typical menstrual period. Ordinarily the amount of menses, or menstrual flow, is not very great, usually no more than five or six tablespoonfuls. The amount of blood that is lost is very sharply limited because natural body processes soon pinch off the vessels that have supplied the uterine lining with blood. This allows the lining of the uterus to return very quickly

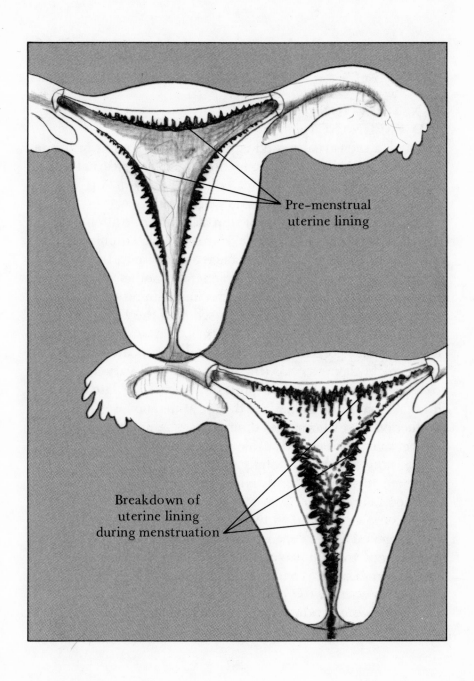

Pre-menstrual
uterine lining

Breakdown of
uterine lining
during menstruation

to its original state, which it will maintain until the next ripened ovum is released.

MENSTRUATION
AND PREGNANCY

All in all, a menstrual period is simply the end point in the female body's attempt at reproduction. That a menstrual period occurs tells us that the attempt failed. The ovum was not fertilized by a sperm, so no pregnancy occurred.

Of course, the body does not stop after just one attempt. Soon after the period is over, the levels of follicle-stimulating hormones from the pituitary gland once again rise in the woman's bloodstream and start the development of another ovum. Estrogens again begin building up in the inner lining of the uterus, the mature ovum is presently released into the Fallopian tube, and the whole ovulation cycle starts once more. If the woman never becomes pregnant, this cycle will be repeated at roughly twenty-eight-day intervals (the exact time will vary a few days from one woman to another) until she reaches her late forties or fifties. At that point in her life, that is, at menopause, a woman's production of sex hormones diminishes, she no longer ovulates, and her menstrual periods come to an end.

The story would be totally different if the mature ovum happened to become fertilized by contact with a sperm. The fertilized ovum would then find its way down into the uterus and become embedded in the special lining of tissue that had been prepared there. Progesterone hormones would continue to be produced to help protect and maintain the pregnancy and would soon stimulate formation of a special organ known as the **placenta** to nourish the growing **embryo.** Soon the placenta itself would begin producing still more progesterone to help protect the pregnancy throughout its term. Because this attempt at reproduction had succeeded, there would be no menstruation. Instead, other hormone-induced signs of pregnancy would begin to appear—breast enlargement, for example, or episodes of nausea. What is more, the progesterone hormones would go to work blocking the development of any new ova until the pregnancy is over, since the woman's body is normally only able to take care of one pregnancy at a time. The woman would not ordinarily begin ovulating again until at least two or three months after the baby was finally delivered, perhaps even longer. And the first evidence that she *was* ovulating again would be the appearance of the first normal menstrual period after her pregnancy was over.

Many women have the idea that since menstruation is so closely related to pregnancy, they can use their menstrual periods to tell when they are likely to become pregnant. Unfortunately, this just doesn't work. It is more accurate to say that menstruation is closely related to *non*pregnancy. Appearance of the menstrual period is usually good evidence that a pregnancy has *not* occurred during the last ovulation cycle. If it had, there wouldn't be any menstrual period. But a normal period tells you nothing whatever about when your body will produce and release its *next* mature ovum. There is no set interval of time between the beginning of a menstrual period and the time of the next ovulation.

Indeed, the only thing that is at all reliable is the amount of time between ovulation and the beginning of the menstrual period that follows—if fertilization hasn't taken place. This is usually about ten days and, within a day or two, applies to most women. Thus, when your period begins, you can look back and say, "Gee, about ten days ago I must have ovulated." But there is no way to pinpoint that critical ovulation day ahead of time.

Perhaps the most important thing to recognize about menstruation is that it is a perfectly normal, logical, and sensible stage in a reproductive cycle that repeats itself over and over again, usually interrupted only when a pregnancy occurs. Now, under ordinary circumstances normal body activities work smoothly and neatly. You rarely see abnormalities appearing. Of course, because you are an individual, your pattern of menstruation will be an individual thing. But the *range of normal* can be very broad. Now that we have seen what menstruation is and why it occurs, we need to consider some of the individual variations that girls may encounter, and see what if anything, they may mean.

Chapter Three:
What's Normal
and What's Not?

Even though menstruation is a normal bodily function, its physical effects can vary a great deal from one person to another. What is more, some girls do indeed experience definite and distressing *ab*normalities with their periods, and almost certainly each one of you will, sooner or later, hear stories about abnormalities that others have experienced. So how on earth can you tell what's normal and what's not?

When problems with menstruation do occur, they are not usually imaginary, or "all in a woman's head." They are very real problems arising for real physical reasons, and in most cases they can be successfully treated. The rest of this chapter should help you decide whether the sensations and feelings you experience in relation to your menstruation are within the range of normal or whether they require attention by a doctor.

TOO EARLY OR TOO LATE

Everything would be much simpler if all girls began menstruating on their thirteenth birthday, but, as we have seen, they don't. There is a range of normal extending from about age eleven through age fourteen. But what about those who begin even earlier or later than this range of normal? These girls are in "problem areas." In most cases nothing whatever is wrong; the girl is simply at the extreme end of the range of normal. But a girl who begins menstruating at age eight or nine, or one who has not menstruated by the time she is fifteen, could have a real physical problem and should have the benefit of a doctor's advice.

What kind of physical problems are we talking about? When they exist, they almost always involve either some kind of hormone disturbance in the body or an anatomical abnormality of some sort—some peculiarity in the physical structure of the body. We have already seen that all the chemical events that trigger the ovulation cycle and keep it humming smoothly are brought about by the action of hormones produced in the ovaries, the pituitary gland, and the adrenal glands. An abnormal growth in any of those glands could change the amount of one or another hormone released into the bloodstream and throw the pattern off. For example, a girl could develop in an ovary a collection of fluid known as a **cyst** that disturbs the organ's functioning and prevents it from producing the right amount of estrogen. On the other hand, the girl might develop in the ovary a small **tumor**—an overgrowth of cells—that produces excessive amounts of estrogen. Either way, the regularity of the ovulation cycle may be disturbed. Similarly, a tumor in the pituitary gland or in the cortex of the adrenal gland might also cause hormone excesses or hormone shortages.

Fortunately, modern medical techniques can pin down such

problems quite rapidly. An ovarian cyst, for example, can often be detected during a simple physical examination. X rays can help the doctor diagnose adrenal or pituitary gland abnormalities, and special laboratory studies of blood and urine known as hormone assays make it possible to tell which hormones, if any, are present in too large or too small a supply. Once the nature of the trouble has been diagnosed, any of these problems can be treated and, usually, cured.

Anatomical malformations—that is, abnormalities in body structure—can also be readily recognized. Perhaps the most common and simple to diagnose malformation is the so-called **imperforate hymen.** In this condition it is the thin sheet of tissue called the **hymen,** or maidenhead, that is causing the problem. Until sexual relations have begun, the hymen normally covers part of the opening to the vagina. But in the case of an imperforate hymen, the tissue actually blocks the outlet altogether, so that there is no way for the menstrual flow to escape. A simple, painless operation in a doctor's office can remove a bit of tissue and solve the problem with no further ado. In more complicated (and extremely rare) cases, a girl may be found to have a **double uterus,** a **double cervix,** or even a **double vagina,** all abnormalities that arose while her body was first developing inside her mother's womb. When such a rare situation is found, expert consultation will point the direction to the best possible treatment.

IRREGULAR OR UNPREDICTABLE MENSTRUATION

While some girls develop a perfectly regular pattern of periods from their first menstrual period on, many girls have quite irregular periods for the first six months, perhaps even for a year or

[33]

two. This can certainly be an annoyance, but usually it doesn't mean anything is wrong. Sometimes, however, an unpredictable pattern just continues indefinitely. In such a case, a visit to the family physician or other doctor may be in order.

Most often irregular periods result from undetectable causes. Minor hormonal imbalances may sometimes, but not always, be at fault. Physical exhaustion or emotional stress at school or at home, very common in the teenage years, is often a contributing factor. If the problem persists, it can usually be cleared up by taking certain hormones orally for an interval of a few months, just long enough to get the menstrual periods established in a regular pattern. Once regulated in this fashion, they usually remain regular.

PAINFUL MENSTRUATION (CRAMPING)

The medical term for any kind of pain or discomfort associated with menstruation is **dysmenorrhea,** from Latin words meaning "difficult menstrual flow." In most cases, however, this refers to the rhythmic painful **cramping** in the lower abdomen that begins just about when the period begins and may continue the entire length of the period.

Some girls get the idea, from talking to others, that practically everybody has painful menstrual cramps. Yet the truth is that many women go through their entire lives without any serious discomfort. On the other hand, most women do experience *some* degree of discomfort during their periods, including mild headaches or backaches, and a small percentage have serious trouble with cramps.

For years a great many doctors thought that women who complained of menstrual cramps were just nuisances. They thought the pain was all in the woman's head, and that since cramping went away when the period was over anyway, there was no need to fuss over it.

Today, however, it is believed that most women who complain of severe cramps are suffering from real physical distress. Tiny hormone-like chemicals called **prostaglandins,** which are produced in the uterus as well as in other organs of the body, may be at fault. No one is yet sure of the exact purpose of these prostaglandins, but we do know that one thing they do in the uterus is to cause uterine muscle fibers to contract. What is more, in many women prostaglandins appear in extremely high concentrations in the uterus shortly after ovulation takes place. Studies have shown that those women who have frequent painful menstrual cramping have a much higher level of prostaglandins in their uterus at menstruation time than do women who have no cramps.

No one yet knows why one woman will have a high level of prostaglandins and consequently suffer from menstrual cramps while another will have a low level and not be bothered at all. However, a variety of medicines are being developed to help block the formation of prostaglandins.

If you have experienced painful cramping or know someone else who has, you may also know that doctors will often prescribe a birth control pill to relieve the symptom. Doctors know that menstrual cramping occurs only in a cycle in which a woman has ovulated. Essentially, oral contraceptives (contraceptive meaning "to prevent pregnancy"), or birth control pills, supply a girl's body with estrogen and progesterone-like hormones that act in such a way to prevent ovulation and, therefore, cramps. The build-up of the inner lining of the uterus and the later loss of cells and blood in the menstrual period

[35]

proceed as usual. But because the pill prevents ovulation, it also prevents cramping when the menstrual period comes.

This kind of medication if used properly is also a highly effective means of preventing pregnancy, since fertilization cannot occur without ovulation. However, birth control pills may have some very dangerous side effects on the body when used over a long period of time, and thus their use for any reason or for any extended period should be considered carefully.

MISSED PERIODS

The medical term for missed periods is **amenorrhea,** meaning, literally, "without menstrual flow." We have already described one kind of amenorrhea, when a girl's first menstrual period is delayed far beyond normal. Another kind can occur when a young woman has been menstruating quite regularly for a period of time and then misses one or more periods.

Of course pregnancy is a very common cause for this second type of amenorrhea. We have seen that if a pregnancy occurs during an ovulation cycle, the expected menstrual period just doesn't occur. Neither does the next nor the next on through the pregnancy. By the time a second period is missed, in such a case, other suggestive signs of pregnancy will also have begun to appear: fullness and tenderness of the breasts, for example, a sense of fullness in the lower abdomen, and often a tendency to feel nauseated in the mornings (morning sickness).

But pregnancy is not by any means the only reason for missing periods. Sometimes they are merely delayed, perhaps because of an illness, severe stress, or a drastic change in diet. Inadequate amounts of protein and iron, sometimes caused by adhering to a poorly planned vegetarian diet, can result not only in missed periods but also in severe **anemia,** a shortage of iron in the blood. Including beans in a vegetarian diet or eggs and milk can prevent this from happening, and a return to a diet providing adequate protein and iron will result in restoring normal periods to a girl's body.

A few women begin missing periods because they have developed a blockage of the cervix. A great many more, however, skip periods for no detectable reason. Often, in such cases, the only thing the doctor can do is to provide treatment with hormones that artificially trigger the menstrual cycle. Once started, menstrual periods in most of these cases resume their normal pattern.

EXCESSIVE
MENSTRUAL FLOW

Within the range of normal that we have spoken of are light menstrual flows that last only three or four days and heavy flows that last five to seven days. In either case, the pattern is usually reasonably consistent from one period to the next. But some women, more often older women but occasionally girls, experience truly excessive, prolonged menstrual flows, a condition known as **menorrhagia.**

Such truly heavy bleeding episodes, especially when they are repeated, require a doctor's attention. They can be disabling, can drain a woman's body of its iron supply, and can cause anemia. Sometimes heavy bleeding episodes are related to the loss of a pregnancy in its early stages (miscarriage). Other times, something may be out of order with the inner lining of the uterus. Even when no cause is determined, there are medications a doctor can prescribe to help control the excessive flow. Any woman who experiences flow far in excess of her usual pattern should not hesitate to see a doctor.

PREMENSTRUAL TENSION

Premenstrual tension, often experienced as depression, head-ache, irritability, or restlessness, is a very complicated condition that frequently precedes the onset of the menstrual period. It seems very much like emotional tension, and emotions are certainly involved. But a wide variety of chemical changes in the body, perhaps over a dozen, are the actual cause. Slight imbalances between estrogen and progesterone after ovulation has taken place may lead to the retention, or holding, of excessively large amounts of salt and water in the body. This gives the woman a bloated, overstuffed feeling. Hormones may also cause soreness of the breasts to occur during this time, which may contribute even further to the emotional tension already present. Recent studies have shown that many women who have severe premenstrual tension also have excessively high levels of prolactin or lactogenic hormone in their bodies. Once the menstrual period begins, however, the offending hormone levels tend to drop off sharply, the kidneys begin releasing the retained salt and water, and the symptoms disappear.

In most women the condition is mild and does not occur with all periods. Merely reducing the amount of salt in the diet for six to eight days before a period is due may be all that is necessary to avoid the symptoms altogether. Or a doctor may prescribe a diuretic—a medicine that forces the kidneys to pass extra salt and water in the urine—starting a week or so before the period. In severe cases, however, medications to lower the levels of prolactin in the woman's body and thus, in many cases, relieve the symptoms, may be prescribed by a doctor.

ENDOMETRIOSIS

Most of the problems of menstruation we've been talking about are not terribly serious. But another disorder, known as **endo-**

[38]

metriosis, is a different matter. This is an extremely painful condition, it does not tend to go away by itself, it can be quite disabling, and it is extremely difficult to treat.

The word comes from *endometrium,* the medical name for the inner lining of the uterus. In most women the menstrual material always flows down and out. But in certain women, for unknown reasons, a small amount of menstrual flow containing cells from the uterine lining tends to back up, moving up the Fallopian tube and escaping out into the lower abdominal cavity outside the uterus. Here clusters of these endometrial cells may become attached to the pelvic region, to the back of the uterus, to the outside of the tube, or to the ovary. The cells then begin to grow on their own, forming little islands of endometrial tissue.

No one knows why this happens in one woman and not in another. Some experts claim it happens more frequently in women whose uterus is tilted slightly back rather than forward. Whatever the cause, once these little islands of endometrial cells have formed outside the uterus, they respond to hormones exactly as if they were still inside. Thus, before ovulation, these clusters of cells begin to grow and enlarge just as the lining of the uterus does. But because of their position, they cause pain, and the larger they get, the more painful they become. Not until menstruation itself occurs, with the uterine lining breaking down and being discharged as menstrual flow, do these islands of endometrial cells begin to shrink so that the pain subsides.

Women with endometriosis often suffer pain in the lower abdomen recurrently month after month. Pregnancy relieves the pain, since there are no ovulation cycles during pregnancy, but these women often have a great deal of difficulty becoming pregnant. The condition can be treated but not always too successfully. In some cases, treatment with hormone combinations, including birth control pills, can relieve the pain substantially.

[39]

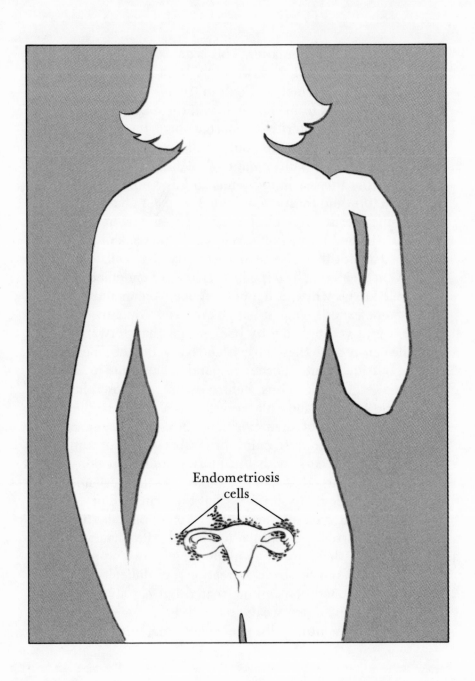

Endometriosis cells

In other cases a lighted instrument known as a laparoscope can be inserted, under anesthesia, into the lower abdomen on a "search and destroy mission" to find the endometrial implants and remove them. So far, however, no fully successful way has been found to cure this condition.

Chapter Four:
Managing Your
Menstruation

T he beginning of menstruation means an obvious change
in your life. Thus, even before your menarche, you should
be aware of the simple, modern ways to take proper care
of your menstrual flow and of the methods available to relieve
any discomfort you experience. You should also know what
physical activities you can continue during your period and
what you might want to avoid. And finally, if any serious menstrual problems do arise, you need to know what doctor to con-
sult and what kinds of examinations he or she will be likely to
perform.

PADS AND TAMPONS
Believe it or not, there was no such thing as a disposable pad
before World War I, just sixty-odd years ago. Items for internal
use are even newer. According to one account, it was an acute

shortage of cotton cloth (used for battle dressings) that led to the invention of the cottony fluff now used in disposable pads.

Most girls, when they start their periods, use **sanitary napkins** —narrow, oblong pads of soft, absorbent stuff wrapped in a porous outer lining—to absorb the flow. Napkins are designed to be worn externally, fitting snugly between the legs. Some are kept in place by a narrow, elastic belt worn around the waist next to the skin and attached to the napkin front and back. But most napkins now have an adhesive strip on the outer surface that effectively attaches the napkin to the panties, thus making a belt unnecessary. Napkins may also contain differing amounts of absorbent material—an extra amount for heavy flow, a smaller amount for mid-period, and so forth.

Napkins should be changed before they become full, an average of four or more times a day during heavy flow, perhaps two or three changes daily toward the end of a period. When removed they should be placed in disposal bags or wrapped in toilet paper and discarded in the trash or garbage. *Never* flush sanitary napkins down the toilet; they will plug up a plumbing system in no time flat.

Although they are handy, tidy, and designed to be form-fitting, napkins do have some disadvantages. They can be bulky and awkward for girls who are physically active; they can't be worn while swimming or bathing; and disposing of them can be a nuisance. **Tampons** were invented to get around these problems. A tampon is nothing more than a small cylinder of expandable, absorbent material designed to be inserted into the vagina during a menstrual period. Once in the vaginal canal, the tampon expands and absorbs the menstrual flow internally. The tampon comes with a good length of string attached, part of which remains outside the vagina so the tampon can be pulled out when it is full.

[43]

Tampons, like napkins, come in various sizes. They are usually easy to insert. Some brands have no applicator. Others come packed inside narrow cardboard or plastic insertion tubes. All you need do is to insert one end of the tampon or tube into the vaginal opening, make sure it is pointed in the right direction and that the string is left to hang free on the outside, and push in on the tampon or inserter end of the tube. Any applicator may then be discarded; the tampon will be placed within the vagina where it belongs.

To get the insertion tube or tampon to enter the body in the right direction—that is, in the same direction as the vaginal canal—you will need at least one of your hips flexed. You can accomplish this by sitting on the toilet seat, spreading your legs, and pointing the tampon or injector at an upward angle toward the small of your back. Or, you can stand with one foot on a chair or with both legs spread and your knees slightly bent while inserting the tampon. Lubrication isn't usually necessary, but it's perfectly okay to use a little cold cream or lubricating jelly to help while you are learning. To remove the tampon, simply pull gently but firmly on the string. Should the string break or otherwise become unusable—and this happens, but only rarely—don't panic. Your fingers will easily be able to reach the tampon and remove it.

Tampons (as well as *cardboard* insertion tubes) may be flushed down the toilet. They should be changed at least twice daily—and remember to remove the last one when your period is ended. Never use more than one tampon at a time. If one is not sufficient protection, try using a combination of napkins and tampons until the flow has lightened.

Many girls have heard they could lose their virginity (that is, break the hymen) by using tampons. This is *very* unlikely to happen. The tampon inserter tip is barely ⅝ inch (1.6 cm) in

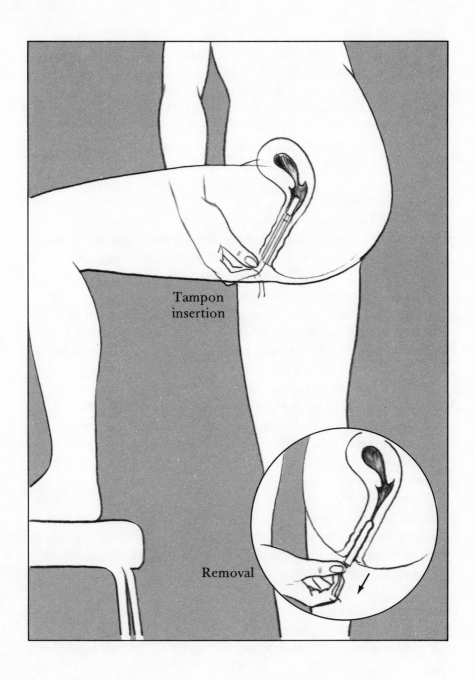

Tampon
insertion

Removal

diameter. Most girls have quite enough space at the vaginal opening to insert this tip right past the hymen with no difficulty. You would have to be extremely rough with yourself to injure this bit of tissue, and, if you were, discomfort would stop you before you did any harm. A few girls really *don't* have the necessary space or can't quite manage to get tampons inserted; these girls should stick with napkins until a doctor can help them.

LIVING THROUGH
YOUR PERIOD

There are only a few things you really should avoid just because of a menstrual period. Fifty years ago menstruating girls were faced with a list of do's and don'ts a mile long—mostly don'ts. Today it's mostly do's.

Bathing. A regular bathing, grooming, and shampooing routine will help you look and feel your best always, and period time is no time to break your routine. If you are using napkins, showers are easiest and cleanest, although tub baths are okay toward the end of a period. Remove your pad before your bath, of course, and replace it with a fresh pad afterward. Water temperature isn't important as long as it's not scalding hot or shockingly cold. Tub baths or showers are fine throughout your period if you have a tampon in place. But change your tampon after a shower or bath.

Swimming. With tampons you can swim or surf anytime without any problem. But if you wear napkins, for reasons of public hygiene you should avoid swimming altogether during a heavy flow, and stay out of pools, hot tubs, and other public bathing areas until your period is over. (Lake or ocean swimming is fine for light days.)

Other sports and activities. Girls no longer have to be wallflowers during their periods. Even the most active sports will do no harm as long as you feel like doing them. In fact, girls who are physically active all month long are less likely to have trouble with menstrual cramps than girls who sit around like lumps all the time. Even as little as a half-hour of brisk walking every day can pay off in more comfortable periods. However don't exhaust yourself, and get plenty of sleep at night. (These last do's and don'ts apply whether you are menstruating or not.)

Diet. There are no good or bad foods for menstruation—no special items you should or shouldn't eat. A balanced diet of nutritious food is good for you any time of the month. You should, however, drink more fluids than normal during periods—eight to ten glasses of water, fruit juice, or milk a day. This will help prevent constipation, a condition that can sometimes contribute to the severity of cramps.

Social activities. Why not? School activities, basketball games, parties, dances—all of the activities you would normally take part in are perfectly fine during menstrual periods, as long as you feel like doing them.

RELIEVING CRAMPS
AND THINGS

Many girls do have cramps or headaches during their periods. Some girls have them just occasionally; others have them quite regularly. Usually these problems are minor and are easily manageable by the girl herself without any professional help. Here are a few tips:

Keeping in shape. Regular, moderate exercise all month long, just keeping your body in reasonable trim, will help prevent cramps and will reduce their severity when they occur. Take plenty of fluids to keep bowel movements regular, as mentioned above.

Medicines. Doctors know that menstrual cramps are caused, at least in part, by prostaglandins produced in the uterus during menstruation. One of the best medicines to reduce prostaglandin

[47]

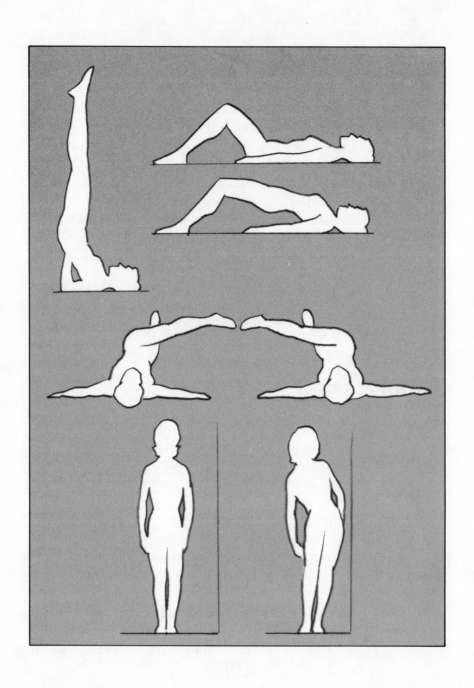

activity is plain aspirin. All the special medicines you see advertised for menstrual distress really contain aspirin as their major ingredient. Two ordinary five-grain aspirin tablets two to three times a day will usually help relieve cramps and headaches as well. *Never take any stronger pain medicine without specific directions from your doctor.*

Physical and mental measures. Sometimes a hot water bottle on the abdomen will help relieve cramps. Use hot tap water, not boiling water, and wrap the bottle in a towel or T-shirt to keep from burning yourself.

Some people claim that "mind over matter" can help, too. If you practice meditation or yoga, try using it to counteract cramps and headaches.

Exercises. A thousand different exercises have been recommended for cramps, which makes it likely that no one of them is consistently helpful. Some, however, may be worth trying. Shoulder stands, for instance, may redistribute or release painful gas bubbles in the intestine and help relieve cramping. Other frequently used exercises include abdominal pumping (back flat, knees bent, push abdomen out during a deep breath, then pull it in sharply as you let the breath out), twisting exercises (back flat, arms out, lift one leg and reach over to touch the floor on the other side with your foot, then back and repeat with the other leg), and the side arc (stand erect, side to the wall about 16 inches (40 cm) away; push hips over to touch the wall, then return to erect position and repeat). Such exercises increase circulation to the pelvis and thus may help to relieve cramps.

THE DOCTOR
IN THE PICTURE

Nobody really *likes* to go to a doctor, but if you are having real and serious menstrual problems—severe and recurrent cramps and pain, for instance, missed periods, or repeated excessive flow—then it's wise to seek professional help.

Three kinds of doctors have experience dealing with menstrual problems. The first is the family physician. He or she encounters such problems frequently and either knows how to treat them or knows what specialist to direct you to. Perhaps more experienced is the specialist in **Obstetrics and Gynecology,** or OB-GYN doctor for short. Obstetrics is concerned with the care of pregnancies; gynecology refers to diagnosis and treatment of disorders of the female reproductive organs. Finally, a fairly new kind of doctor is the modern specialist in Adolescent Medicine.

Today there are many women doctors in all three of these fields; girls who prefer not to have a male doctor examine them would do well to choose one of these. The most important consideration in choosing a doctor, however, aside from professional capabilities, is that you feel relaxed and comfortable with the person.

Any doctor you see about menstrual problems will probably need to perform a **pelvic examination,** sometimes called an internal. No matter what you may have heard, the pelvic exam need not be a particularly painful or distressing experience. The patient, in a loose gown, lies as relaxed as possible on her back on an examining table with knees bent and legs spread. First the doctor makes a brief examination of the external organs, looking for abnormal structures, signs of external infection, rashes, or anything else out of order. Next is the vaginal exam, which requires a narrow instrument shaped like a duckbill and known as a speculum (from words meaning "to look") to be inserted into the vagina. The instrument is warmed and lubricated and a special extra-narrow speculum is used when the patient has never had sexual relations, in order not to disturb the hymen.

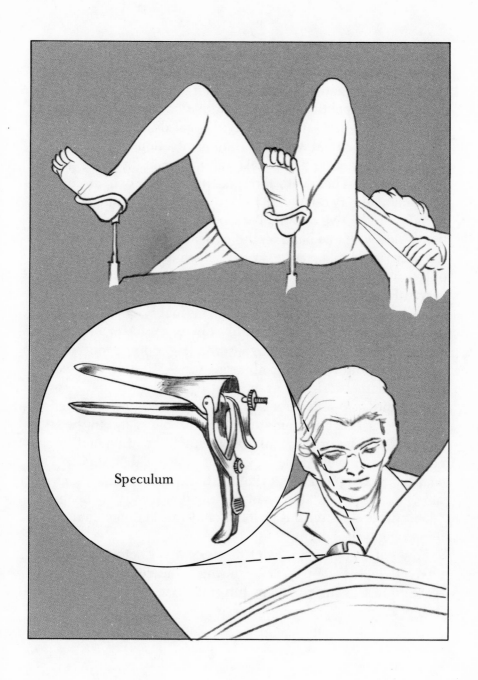

Speculum

When the two paddles of the duckbill are separated slightly, the doctor can see the cervix as well as the inside walls of the vagina. At this time the doctor will often take a **Pap smear** (a few cells scraped from the cervix and vagina) for cancer examination and, if indicated, a sample of any vaginal discharge to examine for possible bacterial, yeast, or fungus infection.

This vaginal examination takes about a minute and is usually quite painless. Then, with the speculum withdrawn, an internal or bi-manual ("two-handed") exam is done to examine the internal reproductive organs. The doctor usually stands at the patient's side with one hand on the patient's lower abdomen. With the other hand in a sterile surgical glove, the doctor inserts one or two fingers into the vagina until the finger meets the patient's cervix. By gently pressing on the abdomen, the doctor can then actually feel the size, shape, and normality of the patient's uterus, ovaries, and Fallopian tubes between his or her fingers. As a final step, the doctor may insert a finger of the gloved hand into the rectum to feel for abnormalities—often a good way to detect endometriosis, for example.

In addition to a pelvic exam, the doctor will carefully check the patient's heart and lungs and the thyroid gland in the front of the neck. The breasts and abdomen will be examined for abnormalities as well. Finally, certain simple lab tests, a blood count, for example, and a urine analysis, will be done. If necessary, more complex lab tests of the blood or urine may be undertaken, depending on the problem and the findings of the preliminary physical exam.

You will certainly not want to seek out a doctor about every minor twinge that may arise during menstruation. But when real and distressing problems turn up, doctors can offer a great deal of help.

[52]

Chapter Five:
Menstruation
in Your Life

From the very beginning we have emphasized that menstruation is a normal, healthy bodily function. But of course it is far more than just that. For each and every one of you, the way you feel about your menstruation, and, in fact, your entire emerging sexuality, will deeply affect your emotional growth and development, your self-image (the picture of yourself that you carry around in your head), your sense of self-esteem (the way you feel about yourself inside), and a dozen other aspects of your life. It will even inevitably affect the way other people regard you.

To get some background on how girls generally feel about menstruation, I spent several evenings at a small college in the Pacific Northwest, talking to a group of a half a dozen college girls. These girls were all between eighteen and twenty years old. They had come from various parts of the country and even from abroad—one girl's home was in Hong Kong. All of them clearly remembered how it was when they had begun menstruating, and all were willing to answer my questions. Here are just a few of the things they said. (The names, of course, have been changed to protect the girls' privacy.)

Q: I've heard it said that many girls find the beginning of menstruation a very distressing or alarming time of life. Were any of you frightened or worried or especially upset at that time?

Sara: Frightened? Not really. I think I felt more of a sense of relief than anything else. From the time I was eleven I kept thinking, "Well, it's going to happen any time now" and then it didn't, and this got to be a drag after a while. And then all of a sudden, there it was, and I sort of thought, "Well, thank God I can quit worrying about it!"

Liu Tang: I think my mother *tried* to scare me, a little. She kept telling me how I was going to have to be very suspicious and careful about boys now, and things like that. But *I* wasn't scared. I wasn't even much interested in boys, at least not for another couple more years.

Q: How did the rest of you feel about boys? Did menstruation make any changes in that?

Sharon: Just that all of them seemed so *young* all of a sudden. Here most of them were still going around with their voices squeaking and busily admiring two hairs on their chins, while I was sprouting out all over. I felt *much* older and more mature. Of course I wasn't, but that's the way I felt.

Mary: I had the feeling that boys were becoming much more wary of *me*. Just a little while before I'd been a real tomboy. I was a better baseball player than any of them, and I could out-swear them all and even slug it out with them if I had to—but then all of a sudden everything changed and we couldn't be pals any more. They got very nervous and self-conscious and wanted to hold hands all the time instead of play baseball. But then, I was a little nervous and self-conscious too. It was like we both had a whole new set of equations to try to figure out and get in balance. Guys had to try to figure out where they fit into those equations, and so did I.

Q: Did you spend a lot of time thinking about this?

Mary: Oh, not much. [Laughing] Just constantly.

Marge: I don't think I thought about it that much. After all, we were all still kids, still just trying our best to figure out how to be adult human beings.

Q: What do you think the boys thought about menstruation?

Marge: Well, most of them seemed to know all about it, or let on that they did. Mostly, I think that they knew something had happened, but most of them weren't quite sure what.

Bev: I remember I was just terribly worried about what the boys thought. Some of the older girls kept telling us how the boys would all avoid you when you were having your period, and how they could tell you were menstruating by looking in your eyes. I even wore dark glasses for a while—talk about a dead giveaway! Of course in a year or so we knew that was all a lot of nonsense.

Sara: I heard those things, too, but they didn't bother me. But then I was pretty bashful in those days. I had a lot of acne and thought I was just grotesquely ugly, so I pretended I didn't *care* what the boys thought.

Q: Earlier one or two of you spoke of your periods with a certain amount of annoyance or even anger. I think it was Liu Tang who said they were a "big fat bother." Do any of you actually *enjoy* anything about having periods? Do you think they provide any sort of an advantage?

Mary: Oh yes! There's no question about it. It's hard to put it

[55]

into words, but I think there's a certain comfortable feeling of *rightness* about things when your period comes. It's as if your body is sending you nice loud signals that you're in good shape and everything is working the way it should. You're a whole, complete person.

Sharon: It does give you a sense that things are all right, maybe a sense of maturity, too.

Q: One last question: I've heard people say that menstruation makes a girl a woman. What do you think about that?

Mary: Well, now, just hold it a minute. [She chewed her lip for a long time.] That certainly doesn't sound right to *me*. Haven't you got it backwards?

Sara: You might say that *ovulating* makes a girl a woman because then she can get pregnant—but does just being able to get pregnant make a girl a woman? I don't think menstruation makes you *anything* in particular.

Marge: I'm not sure that getting pregnant necessarily makes you a woman either. What about the thirteen and fourteen year old girls that get pregnant? I don't think they're *women*, pregnant or not. They're just teenage girls who've gotten pregnant.

But all the girls agreed that Sharon gave the best answer of all:

Sharon: Of course all by itself it doesn't make you a woman. It couldn't. Really, menstruation is just telling you that your body has become sexually mature enough so that you're capable of having a baby. That's *part* of being a woman, and a very important part, too, but that isn't all there is to it. It seems to me that menstruation is just one of a whole flock of signals a girl gets in her early teens that tells her she's beginning to develop into a mature woman and she'd better start getting ready for it. Menstruation says, *things are changing—better pay attention*.

[56]

But really, becoming a mature woman involves a million other things too—learning how to be responsible for what you do, learning to make your word good so that other people can always count on it, developing good judgment and learning how to use it, learning how to develop really mature, responsible relationships with men—a million other things work into the picture.

A million other things indeed. If nothing else, we have seen how many different patterns menstruation alone can take. No one can say to you, "This is what is going to happen to you when you begin menstruating." There is too much variation from one person to the next, all within the range of normal. Menstruation is an *individual* matter, and it is just one part of a Grand Pattern of physical and emotional events that occurs as you leave your childhood behind and steadily develop into an adult.

Glossary of
Important Terms

(*Note*. Specific organs of the male and female body are not included in this glossary. Definitions and illustrations of them may be found by referring to the index.)

Acne: Pimples; a skin disorder related to androgens in the body.

Amenorrhea: Medical term for missed periods.

Androgens: The male sex hormones produced mainly in the testes and the cortex of the adrenal gland.

Anemia: A shortage of iron in the blood.

Cramping: Discomfort or pain sometimes felt in the lower abdomen during menstrual periods. Caused by contractions of muscle fibers in the uterus.

Cyst: A collection of fluid; if formed on an ovary, may throw a period off.

Dysmenorrhea: The medical term for any period discomfort, but usually refers to cramping.

Embryo: A baby in its early developing stages. The embryo usually lodges and grows inside the uterus.

Endometriosis: A serious, painful disorder related to a disturbance in the menstrual flow.

Estrogens: Female sex hormones produced mainly in the ovaries.

Female reproductive cycle: The entire cycle, controlled by hormones, during which the female becomes prepared for pregnancy.

Fertilization: The penetration of a ripe ovum by a sperm cell. The two cells fuse together and then develop into an embryo.

Follicle-stimulating hormone (FSH): A hormone from the pituitary gland that helps stimulate the ripening of an ovum in a woman's ovary.

Growth spurt: The increase in body growth that occurs at the time of sexual maturation, usually between ages eleven and fourteen.

Hormones: Chemical substances formed in certain glands and organs of the body and carried by the bloodstream to affect the behavior of other organs.

Imperforate hymen: A rare malformation of the tissue that normally covers part of the opening to the vagina in females who have not yet had sexual relations.

Lactogenic hormone: The hormone that works with estrogens to enlarge a woman's breasts and make them milk-producers.

Luteinizing hormone (LH): The hormone used to help form the corpus luteum tissue in the ovary during ovulation.

Menarche: A girl's first menstrual period.

Menopause: The time of life, usually around age fifty, when a woman no longer produces reproductive cells and ceases to have menstrual periods.

Menorrhagia: An excessive, prolonged menstrual flow.

Menses: The cellular material and blood that passes out of the body during a menstrual period. More commonly known as the menstrual flow.

Menstruation: The shedding of cells from the uterine lining, together with some blood, which occurs when a female egg cell has not been fertilized.

Mittelschmerz: Twinges of discomfort in the lower abdomen occasionally felt by some women during ovulation.

Obstetrics and gynecology (OB-GYN): The medical specialty of treating disorders of the female reproductive organs and pregnancies.

Ovulation: The release of a ripened ovum from the ovary where it was formed. Upon release it travels down the Fallopian tube toward the uterus.

Ovum (pl. Ova): A female reproductive cell, the egg cell.

Pap smear: A scraping of cells from the vagina and cervix, used to determine if cancer is present.

Pelvic examination: The usual examination doctors perform to check for diseases or abnormalities of the female reproductive organs.

Period: The menstrual period, that is, the interval of days approximately every four weeks when menstruation takes place.

Placenta: The special organ that grows within the uterus during pregnancy to help the body supply oxygen and nutrients to a growing baby.

Premenstrual tension: The emotional and physical changes often experienced just prior to or at the beginning of menstrual periods. Premenstrual tension is caused by hormones in the body.

Progesterone: A female sex hormone that helps support the ovum until it is fertilized and protects the growth of the new baby if pregnancy occurs.

[60]

Prolactin: Another name for lactogenic hormone.

Prostaglandins: Hormones manufactured in the uterus (among other places) that sometimes produce menstrual cramping.

Puberty: The time of sexual maturation; that is, the time when both males and females become physically able to reproduce.

Sanitary napkins: Narrow, oblong pads of absorbent cottony material used to absorb menstrual flow externally.

Secondary sex characteristics: Those bodily manifestations of sex not directly related to reproduction but which essentially prepare the body for it.

Sperm: A male reproductive cell. Has a long, whiplike tail.

Tampon: A narrow, compressed cylinder of absorbent material designed to be inserted into the vagina to absorb menstrual flow internally.

Tumor: An overgrowth of cells which, if it forms on an ovary, can throw off a period.

Index

[63]

Oral contraceptives, 35–36, 39
Ovaries, 14, 19, 25, 52
    cysts in, 32
    tumors in, 32
Ovulation, 21, 26, 29, 36, 60
Ovulation cycle, 19–26, 29
Ovum, 19, 21, 26, 28, 60

Pap smear, 52, 60
Pelvic examination, 50, 60
Period, 26, 60
    discomfort during, 34–35
    irregular pattern of, 33–34
    length of, 5, 6
    missed, 36–37
    See also Menstruation
Physical activity, 9, 46–47
Physical exhaustion, 34
Pituitary gland, 14, 21, 25, 28
    tumors in, 32
Placenta, 28
Pregnancy, 6, 18, 19, 28, 36
    and endometriosis, 39
Premenstrual tension, 38, 60
Progesterone, 25, 26, 28, 29, 60
    imbalance, 38
Prolactin, 25, 38, 61
Prostaglandins, 35, 47–49, 61
Protein, 36, 37
Puberty, 6, 21, 61
Pubic hair, 17

Reproduction, 19
Reproductive cycle, 13

Salt retention, 38
Sanitary napkins, 42, 43, 61
Secondary sex characteristics, 17, 61
Self-image, 53

Sex glands, 14
Sex hormones, 17, 18, 19
Sexual maturity, 18, 19
Sexual relations, 19
Skin, 18
Sleep, 47
Speculum, 50, 52
Sperm, 19, 21, 28, 61
Sports, 9, 46–47
Stress, 34
Swimming, 46

Tampons, 42–46, 61
Testicles, 14, 18, 19
Thyroid gland, 52
Tumor, 32, 61

Underarm hair, 17, 18
Urine analysis, 52
Uterine lining, 25, 26–27
    during pregnancy, 28
    excessive menstrual flow, 37
Uterus, 5, 35, 52

Vagina, 5
    double, 33
Vaginal discharge, 52
Vaginal exam, 50–52
Vegetarian diet, 36–37
Voice, 14, 17, 18

Walking, 47
Water retention, 38
Weight, 9

X-rays, 33

Yeast infection, 52
Yoga, 49